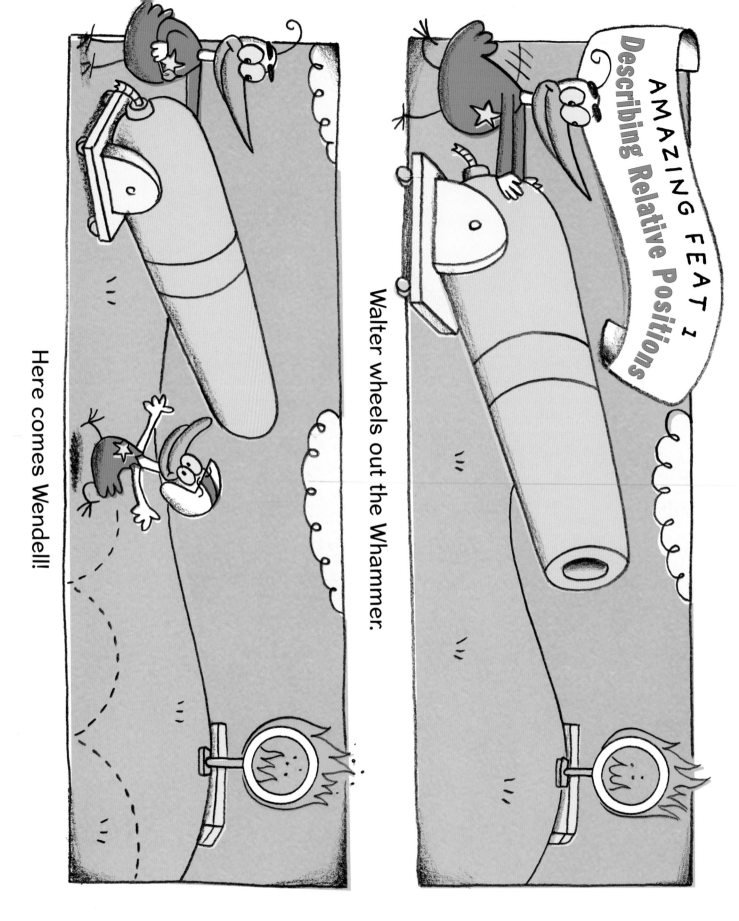

Walter wheels out the Whammer.

Here comes Wendell!

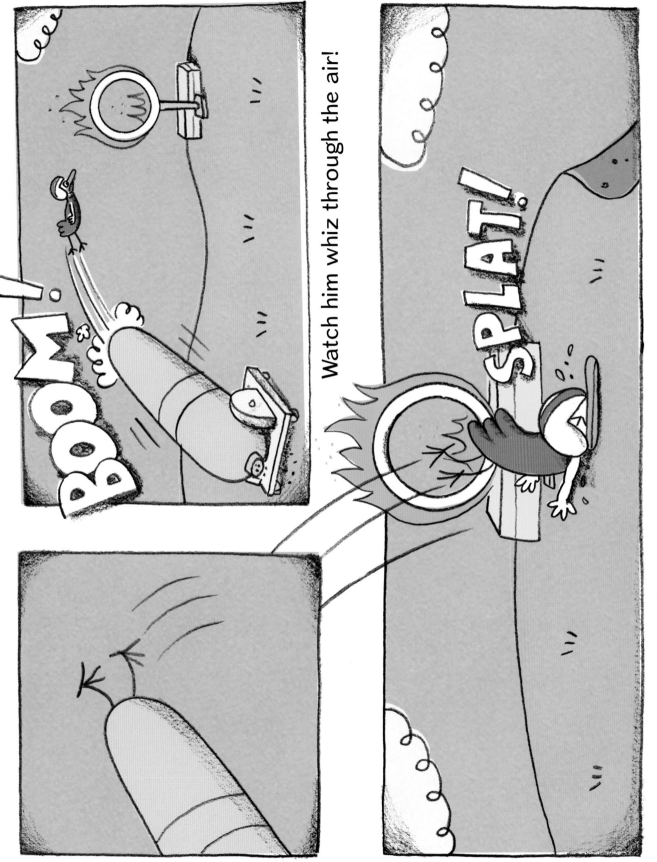

Watch him whiz through the air!

Wendell lands IN FRONT OF the Circle of Fire.

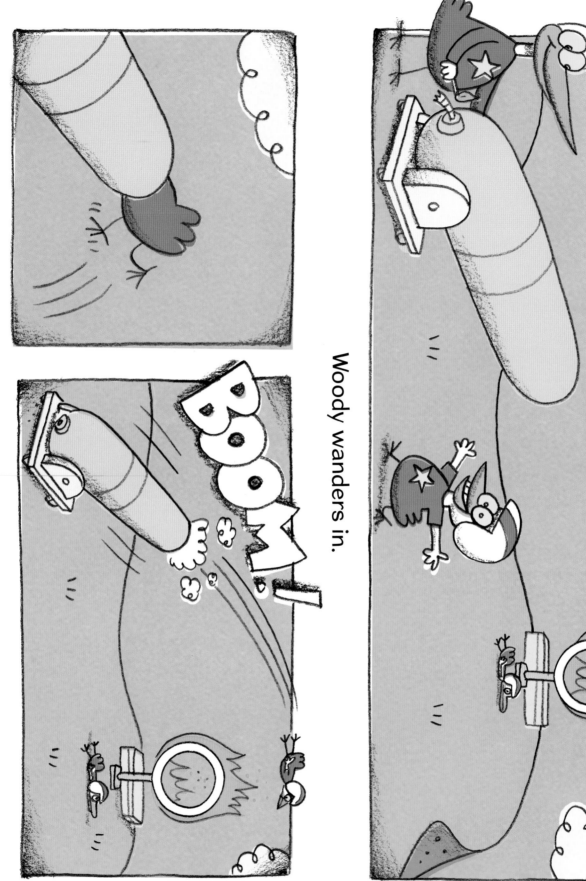

He whistles ABOVE the Circle of Fire . . .

Woody wanders in.

BOOM!

. . . and lands BEHIND it.

Wilmer wants to try.

Wilmer lands BESIDE the Circle of Fire.

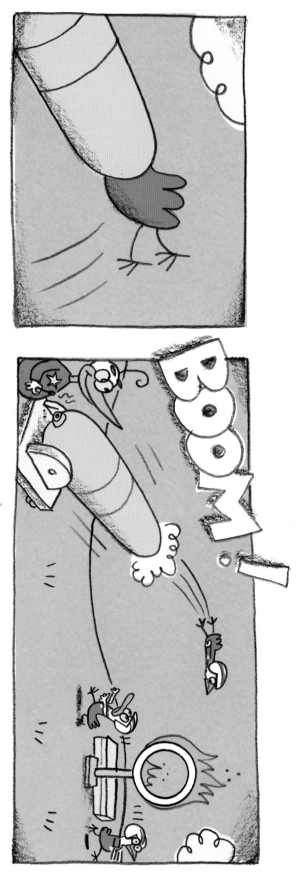

Of course, Willy wants to be the winner.

But he is way off! He lands BELOW the Circle of Fire!

Which, of course, leaves Walter.

Walter is ABOVE the Circle of Fire! WAY ABOVE!

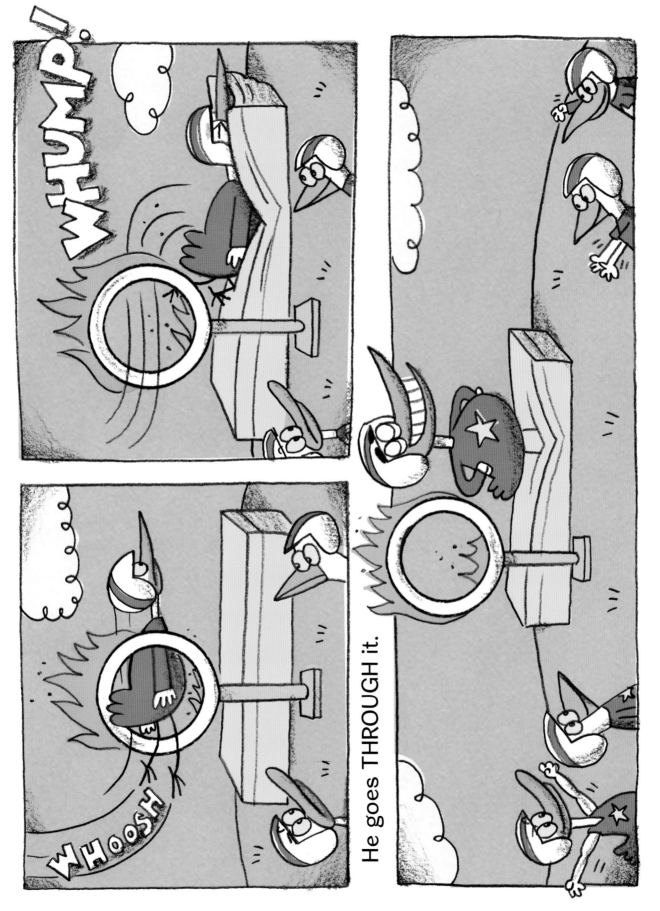

He goes THROUGH it.

Wow, Walter! Way to go!

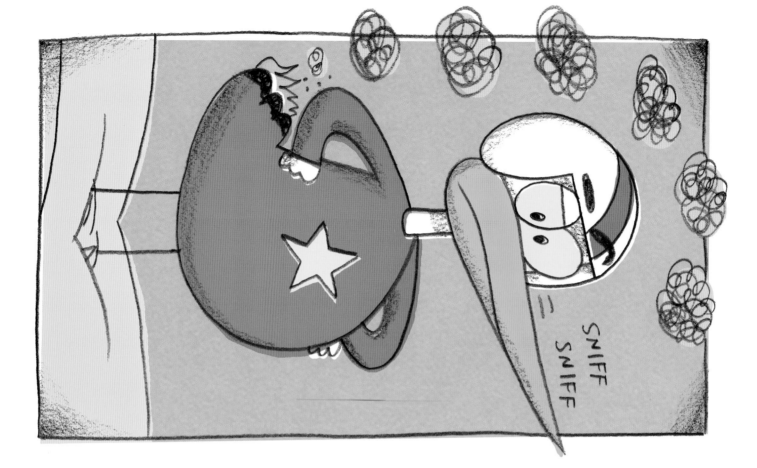

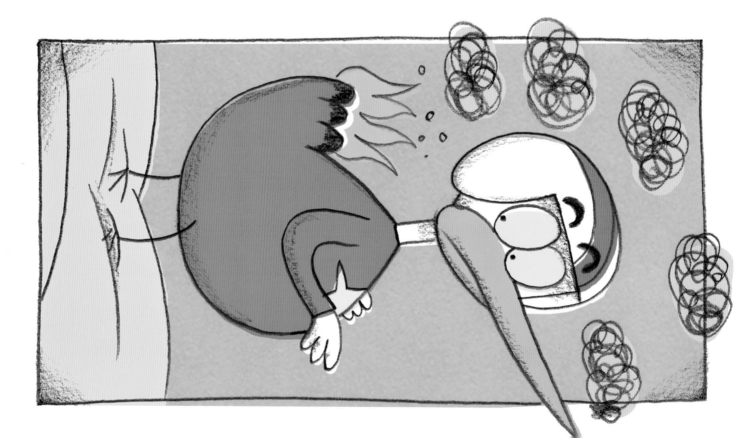

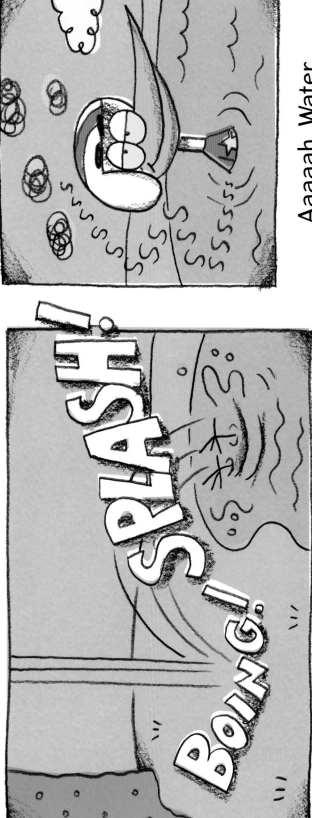

What is Walter doing with that wand?

It's a triangle!

It's a square!

Gee whiz, Walter, that is some wand!

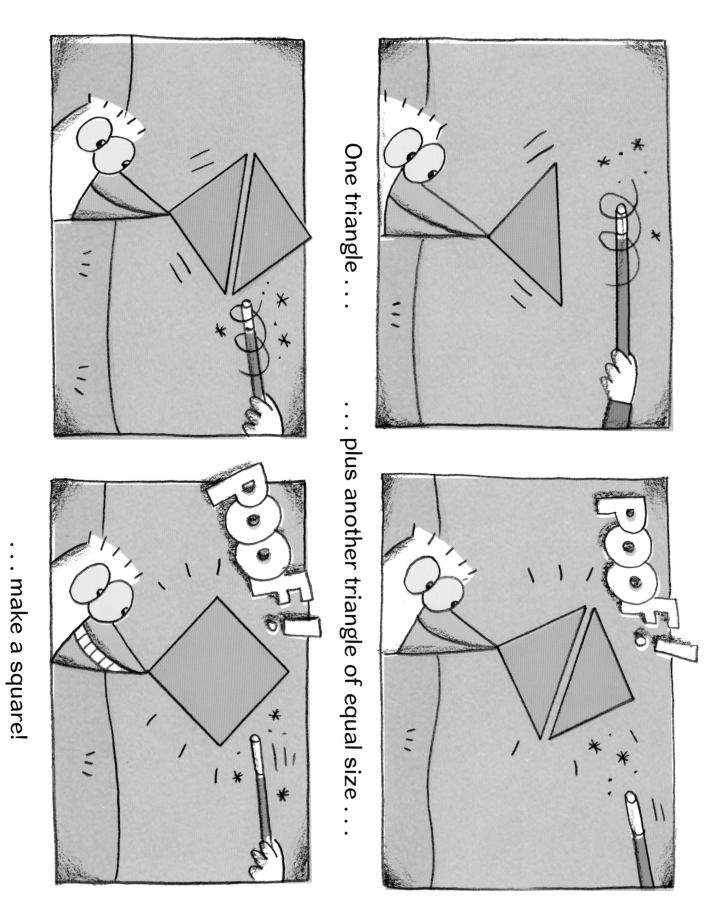

One triangle . . .

. . . plus another triangle of equal size . . .

. . . make a square!

One square . . . . . . plus another square of equal size . . . . . . make a rectangle!

Wow, Walter! You are a wizard with that wand!

One square plus two triangles of equal size can make . . . a parallelogram!

One rectangle plus two triangles of equal size can make . . . a trapezoid!

Whoa, that wand is wild, Walter!

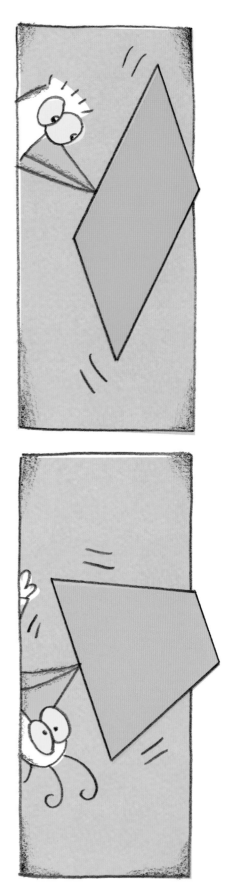

Woody and Wilmer are a little wobbly.

Watch out, Walter!

Walter, your legs look a little out of whack.

Walter, you need little west.

Walter is in a wooden box. Wendell draws lines to divide the box into equal parts.

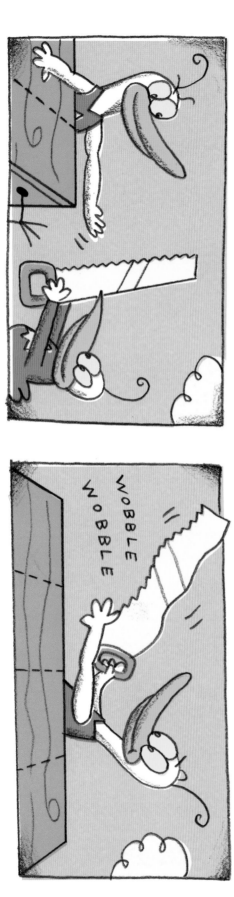

Wendell wants his saw. He will saw the box into two halves.

Walter's head will stick out of one-half of the box.

Walter's feet will stick out of the other half of the box.

The box is in two equal parts.

Now Wendell will cut the box into fourths, which are also called quarters. Walter's head will stick out of one-fourth of the box.

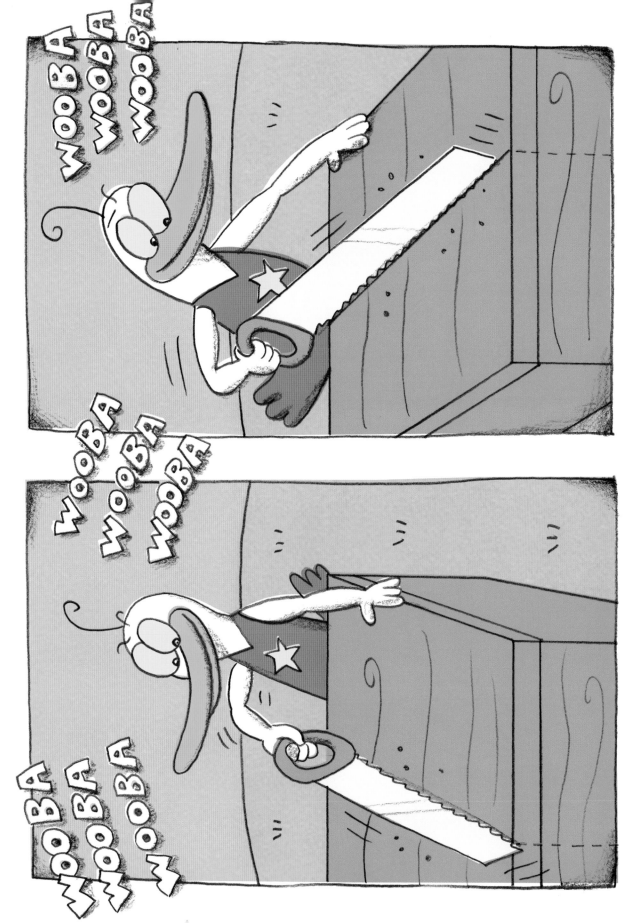

His wings will be in one-fourth of the box.
His feet will stick out of another quarter of the box.

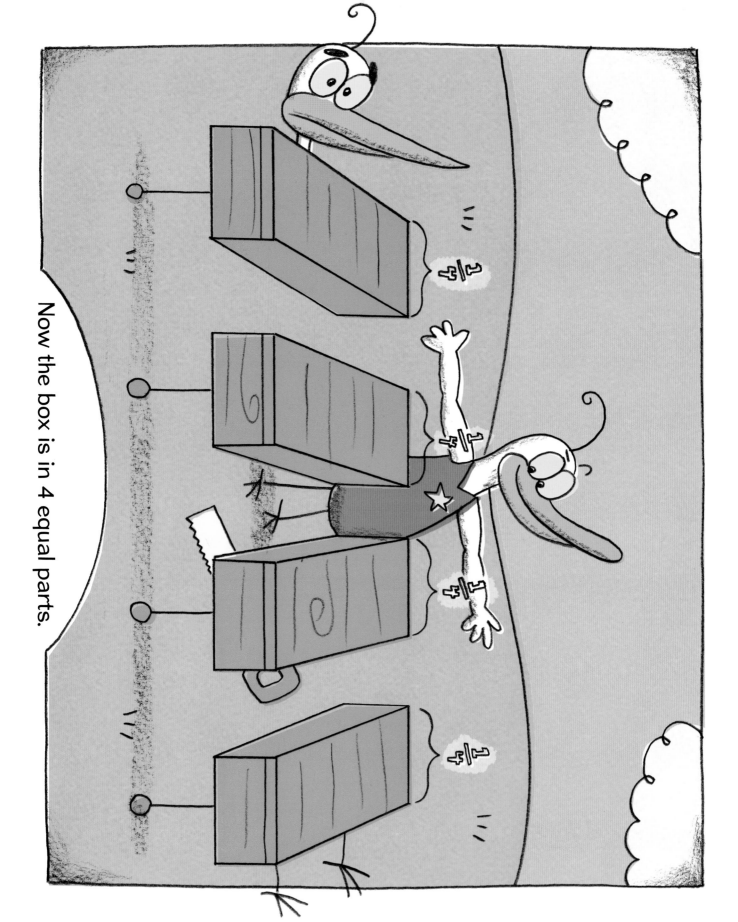

Now the box is in 4 equal parts.

Wahoo! Walter is in one whole piece! So is the box.

Wing Wing brothers, take a bow!

WHUMP! WHUMP! WHUMP!

Oh, NO! Walter is in wedges!

What will the Wing Wing brothers do now?!

The Common Core State Standards

This book meets the Common Core State Standards for kindergarten mathematics in Geometry: K.G.A.1 and K.G.B.6. It also meets the Common Core State Standards for first-grade mathematics in Geometry: 1.G.1.3.

The publisher would like to thank Bruce R. Vogeli, PhD, Clifford Brewster Upton Professor and Director, Program in Mathematics, Teachers College, Columbia University, for his expert reading of the text and sketches for this book.

To my brothers, Alec, Mark, and Matt.
And my sister Ashley

—E. L.

HOLIDAY HOUSE is registered in the U.S. Patent and Trademark Office.
Printed and Bound in November 2013 at Tien Wah Press, Johor Bahru, Johor, Malaysia.
The artwork was created with black Prismacolor pencils on bristol board and colored digitally on a Mac.
www.holidayhouse.com
First Edition
1 3 5 7 9 10 8 6 4 2

Library of Congress Cataloging-in-Publication Data
Long, Ethan.
The Wing Wing brothers geometry palooza! / by Ethan Long. — First edition.
pages cm.
Audience: Age 3 to 6.
ISBN 978-0-8234-2951-6 (hardcover)
1. Geometry—Juvenile literature. I. Title.
II. Title: Geometry palooza.
QA445.5.L65 2014
516—dc23
2013016435